SPEAKING WITHOUT WORDS

SPEAKING WITHOUT WORDS

The story of Rachel's stroke

Marjorie Durward
Yolande Crowe
Jane Marshall
Jo Robson

Illustrations by Alice Englander

La Borie
2000

Published in 2000 La Borie
220 Cranmer Court London SW3 3HG

Copyright © Marjorie Durward 2000
Illustration copyright © Alice Englander

ISBN 0-9538196-0-4

A catalogue record for this book is available from the British Library

Typeset in New Century 12/14pt
by Scriptmate Editions

Manufacture coordinated in UK by
Book-in-Hand Ltd, 20 Shepherds Hill, London N6 5AH

All rights reserved. No part of this book may be reproduced or transmitted in any form, electronic or mechanical, including photocopy or any information storage and retrieval system, without permission in writing from the publisher.

Introduction

Through the early weeks of 1993 Rachel, who was then in her mid-seventies, frequently mentioned feeling tired but she continued to work steadily until late spring when she had a massive stroke. This ended a long and distinguished academic career.

Rachel was admitted to a large National Health Service hospital in London where she was found to have extensive damage to the left side of her brain. As a result her right arm and leg were paralysed. But a far more serious consequence of the stroke was her totally incomprehensible speech. Rachel had aphasia.

Both the doctors and the speech and language therapists explained that Rachel's aphasia was the result of brain damage and, as she had a very serious type of aphasia known as jargon aphasia there was virtually no hope of improvement. Furthermore, it was assumed that Rachel's understanding would be as seriously affected as her speech.

What was aphasia? What was jargon aphasia? How could Rachel be helped and who could provide that help?

This book is the story of Rachel's life after her

stroke. It is also the story of our friendship with Rachel since then, a period which has been both harrowing and occasionally hilarious, both frustrating and fascinating. And it is the story of her speech and language therapy with Jane Marshall and Jo Robson who included Rachel in a Medical Research Council project. We hope that our combined voices will strike a chord with others who live or work with aphasic people.

Contents

What is Aphasia?	9
'Is it getting better?' The Story of Rachel's Stroke	15

'I'm sorry, I don't understand you':
     Rachel's Communication Skills
     and Difficulties
	30

Making Progress Therapy with Rachel	46
'What do you do when she laughs?' Friends, visitors and staff	59
Living with Dignity after Stroke The Long Term	67
Final Thoughts	77
Glossary	79
Bibliography	87
Helpful Organisations	89

What is Aphasia?

Aphasia* is a language disorder arising from brain damage, the most common causes being stroke and head injury. Aphasia disrupts all aspects of language. This means that aphasic people have difficulty talking, reading, writing and understanding speech. They may also have problems with non-verbal communication, such as gesture or drawing.

Although language is disturbed in aphasia, other mental skills are not. Aphasic people can still remember, think and reason. So they will recall the main events in their life, be able to work out problems and retain their political views (even though they may not be able to express those views). Likewise, aphasia itself does not change the individual's personality. If they liked football before their stroke, they will like it afterwards.

One of the striking features of aphasia is its variability. Indeed no two aphasic people have quite the

* Acquired language disorder can be referred to as aphasia or dysphasia. Technically, aphasia means the total loss of language, while dysphasia means its partial loss. In practice, the terms tend to be used interchangeably. Throughout this book we have plumped for the term aphasia.

same problems. This is illustrated by the following samples.

> *Speaker 1* (describing the events of her weekend)
> Mother's day ... er ... Nichola ... meals ... flowers ... er chocolates
>
> *Speaker 2* (describing a dog)
> Hangs about the place ... got two horses and a tail and the mouth changes from various aspects of the bird
>
> *Speaker 3* (saying that he will go to the park in the afternoon)
> we have to go to the pargoney
>
> *Speaker 4* (asked if she had been out)
> yes, butter gid a mine eye dort igerdermernye norter wun gudermini midi dermunight

The first person talks very hesitantly. Her speech contains no verbs, no sentences and no grammatical words (like 'the' or 'was'). As a result, this type of speech is sometimes called 'agrammatic'. Despite this, speaker 1 has some success communicating the events of her weekend, mainly because she can produce relevant nouns.

Speaker 2 is different. His speech is fluent, grammatical and contains plenty of verbs. However, this person is still very difficult to understand. One reason for this is the problem with nouns. So, in the quoted sample, he says 'horses' instead of 'ears' and on another occasion he called a 'crutch' a 'superwalk'. As these examples show, his mistakes often bear some relationship to the target.

The first two speakers use mainly real words. This is not the case for speakers 3 and 4, both of whom produce nonsense words, or neologisms. Indeed, speaker 4 produces virtually nothing but neologisms.

The last three speakers all have Jargon Aphasia. In this form of aphasia, speech is fluent or even copious. It may also be grammatical or, at least, preserve a normal intonation line. For this reason, jargon speakers often sound as if they are talking normally, particularly when heard from a distance. It is only when the listener gets close to them, that the peculiarity of their speech becomes obvious. As the samples show, jargon speech varies. In some cases, as with speaker 2, the person uses mainly real words, albeit in rather odd combinations. In others, neologisms predominate. Speaker 4 is Rachel, the subject of this book. As the sample shows her speech consisted of incomprehensible strings of nonsense words.

Speech is not the only problem in jargon aphasia. Most people also have a severe comprehension disorder, or cannot understand what is said to them. The extent of this difficulty varies. Some people have virtually no comprehension, in which case they may believe that everyone round them is talking in a foreign language. Others have a much milder difficulty, which only causes them to miss the odd word. This seemed to be the case for Rachel. Reading and writing are also commonly impaired in jargon aphasia, although again the patterns vary. Some jargon speakers also produce fluent but meaningless writing; while others, like Rachel, struggle even to write one word.

Perhaps the most surprising feature of jargon aphasia is the self — monitoring problem, in that many people seem totally unaware that their speech is at all disrupted. They carry on talking as if they are making perfect sense and expect relatives and friends to reply. When not understood, they become puzzled or furious, and may even suspect relatives of conducting some form of conspiracy against them. This oblivion can make the person very resistant to speech and language therapy. They simply cannot see that there is a problem to be addressed.

The sheer oddity of jargon aphasia can generate a number of myths and misunderstandings. One is that the person is confused, or even mentally ill. Indeed, some people with jargon aphasia have been committed to psychiatric institutions, before the correct diagnosis is achieved. However, as in other forms of aphasia, people with jargon speech are still mentally intact. Rachel retained her knowledge about art and was able to demonstrate this by pointing appropriately to pictures in books and catalogues. She also developed clever strategies and skills to cope with her overwhelming communication problems.

Another common myth is that jargon speakers may be using some form of code. In other words, care staff or friends may believe that the person has generated a new vocabulary which has replaced conventional language. Unfortunately this is not the case (if it were, we would simply have to crack their code in order to restore communication). Rather, the mistakes made in jargon are very inconsistent. Thus the person might call a telephone a 'pidlum' on one occasion and a 'tanktop' on the next. A variant on this misunderstanding is that the person is using an unfamiliar foreign language. One woman, known to the authors, was thought by ward staff to have reverted to her first language after her stroke, which was Welsh. It was only when she was assessed by a Welsh speech and language therapist, that she was identified as having jargon aphasia.

All forms of aphasia are extremely distressing. Aphasic people report feelings of loneliness, fear, frustration and anger. These feelings are shared by friends and relatives, who also struggle to cope with the effects of aphasia and desperately miss their previous communication with the aphasic person. Arguably, jargon aphasia is the most difficult form of aphasia to live with. Jargon speakers are often completely incomprehensible and may understand little of what is said to them. Furthermore, the lack of awareness can generate huge friction within the home. They too must feel distressing emotions, yet lack the language to express them. Unsurprisingly, friends and relatives can feel completely at a loss when trying to deal with the problems.

> 'Is frightened. Is frightened'.

> 'It was like hitting somewhere at 100 miles per hour'

> 'Big cot. All fence ... fenced me around'

> 'I was desperate because I thought 'My God ... what about my job?'

> 'I was mad. I was mad in here that it wouldn't come

> out — when I did try to say to something um ... and it all come out ... well gobbledegook ... um ... and I knew what I was going to say but I couldn't say it and I used to get mad — Mad with myself.[*]

We, too, were just as flummoxed by Rachel's jargon and although we have gained a few insights along the way, we remain almost as puzzled today as we were when the stroke first happened. Perhaps, what we have gained is some ideas about how to cope with the problems, despite our poor understanding.

The following sections describe the events after Rachel's stroke, her communication difficulties and the content of her therapy. We also discuss some of the reactions of those in contact with Rachel and finally reflect on the long term issues of living with jargon aphasia.

---

[*] Parr S, Byng S, and Gilpin S, *Talking about Aphasia: Living with Loss of Language after Stroke.* Milton Keynes: Open University Press (1997).

'Is it getting better?'
The Story of Rachel's Stroke

Early Days

It was teatime on a Thursday in May when Rachel had a stroke. We knew this because we found the tea pot and the little Chinese cup on a small table beside her armchair. And we listened to the messages left on the answering machine. On the following Monday a neighbour returned from a few days in the country and found several newspapers delivered for Rachel lying in the communal hall. He noticed that Rachel's bedroom window was open and, suspecting something was amiss, rang first her door bell and then her telephone number. Getting no reply to either, he rang the police who broke into her flat. Rachel was lying on her sitting room floor. The police called for an ambulance and she was taken to a large general hospital.

The following morning when I walked into the ward Rachel, who was sitting by her bed attached to various tubes and drips, raised her left hand and pointed a finger towards me. As I walked across the ward Rachel continued to point. There could be no doubt that she had both seen and recognised me, although she was without her spectacles. On reaching her bedside I discovered that Rachel's right arm and leg were paralysed and her speech a meaningless babble.

One can only assume that the continuous, undifferentiated babble with which Rachel greeted me was an attempt to explain her predicament. No one will ever know her thoughts at this or any other time. However, others who have regained their ability to speak intelligibly, have talked and written movingly about their initial confusion, of their overwhelming fear and of their great weariness. They say that although they often talked incessantly, they were not aware that their speech made no sense at all.

A few days after being admitted to hospital, Rachel was seen by a speech and language therapist. The curtains were drawn round her bed and I waited for the verdict. How much improvement could we expect in the weeks ahead? Would Rachel ever be able to speak normally again?

When the speech and language therapist emerged from behind the curtains, she said that Rachel could swallow. While this was important information, as it meant that the tubes could be removed and that Rachel could eat and drink normally, it was not the information I was expecting. I had been hoping for an expert opinion on Rachel's speech and it had not occurred to me that her ability to swallow would be assessed by a speech and language therapist. However, from brief conversations with the therapist during the following week it became clear that it was most unlikely that Rachel would regain normal speech. We were advised to discourage her babbling and told that the nurses at the rehabilitation centre, to which she would soon be moved, were specially trained to deal with speech problems.

Rachel's transfer to the Rehabilitation Centre

After two weeks in hospital, arrangements were made for Rachel to transfer to a rehabilitation centre. When this was explained to her, she appeared to understand and to be interested. As the exact time of the transfer depended on the Ambulance Service, the Charge Nurse sensibly suggested that we should stay at home and that she would telephone to tell us when Rachel had left the ward. She duly made this call at 2.40pm, and we took a taxi to the Rehabilitation Centre in order to meet Rachel who was expected to arrive at about 3pm.

When Rachel had not arrived by 4pm we were not particularly concerned because the staff explained that the ambulance would probably call at other places before bringing Rachel to the Centre. However, a member of the staff telephoned the hospital and was assured that Rachel had left as planned. At 6pm another telephone call to the hospital confirmed that Rachel had left the ward at 2.40pm. By now we were becoming increasingly concerned about Rachel because even if nothing untoward had happened, it would be impossible for her to ask questions and it was unlikely that anyone would have time to explain to her the cause of the delay.

At 8pm there was still no sign of Rachel. Although reassured by the staff at the Rehabilitation Centre, who said that patients were sometimes taken to the depot and transferred to another ambulance, we were seriously concerned. However reasonable the explanation, a delay of five hours must be causing Rachel great anxiety. The staff were asked to check again and this time the Charge Nurse enquired at the Ambulance depot and discovered that no one knew anything about Rachel. The Ambulance service made further calls and eventually we were told that Rachel was still sitting in a wheelchair in the casualty department of the hospital waiting to be collected. An ambulance was sent for her at once and she arrived at the Rehabilitation Centre at 8.45 pm, cold, tired, hungry and in considerable distress.

Such confusion illustrates the need for improved communication within the hospital. It also illustrates the need for special arrangements when dealing with aphasic people. It would have been impossible for Rachel to ask for help or information because even if she had attracted attention, no one would have understood her jargon. Perhaps a highly visible notice attached to her wheelchair giving her name and instructions for the Ambulance Service might have alerted a passing nurse to her plight.

The next step

As early as the second week after her stroke Rachel occasionally used real words. For instance, she sometimes exclaimed 'No', and often said 'I don't know ...' in a bewildered tone. Once, rather sadly, she asked 'Is it getting better?'. Very gradually the spate of monotone jargon decreased and normal speech rhythms and intonation appeared. Now, even though most of her words remained incomprehensible, we could tell from her intonation whether she was asking a question, making a comment or thundering out a complaint.

Although she tired very quickly, we tried to maintain Rachel's interest in her life before her stroke. She was shown photographs, journals and magazines and we talked about everyday activities. It was while looking with interest at a 'Birds' magazine that she pointed to a picture of a handsome Kingfisher and said 'Fish-kinger'. Rachel always listened very carefully to explanations and responded with both jargon and words. When I explained that I was going to Paris for a few days Rachel said 'Miss you', and when a favourite care worker returned after a long break she cried out happily 'You've come back'. Visitors noticed Rachel listened to conversations about people and places and by the occasional recognisable word she indicated that she had grasped at least the gist of what was being discussed.

The occasional words and phrases convinced us that Rachel understood much of what was being said. Consequently, we were troubled by the advice of the speech and language therapist who insisted that Rachel understood very little and that her 'talking' must be stopped. For us, Rachel's talking was informative. From her tone of voice, and the admittedly infrequent real word, it was possible to find clues about what was causing her concern. We could then give her explanations which undoubtedly helped to relieve her mounting anxiety. For example, when I visited Rachel one morning she was in evident distress with the words 'terrible ... terrible ... papers' appearing in her jargon. Although she could not tell me what the problem was, I guessed that she might be referring to one of the many learned societies with which she was involved. Fortunately, my guess was right and I was able to reassure her and explain to her our plans for taking care of her affairs.

As she became more aware of her situation there was ample evidence that Rachel's strong personality and her sense of humour remained intact. Her ability to fit in socially was apparent when still at the Rehabilitation Centre. She appreciated visitors, listened to conversations and never interrupted. She laughed merrily and appropriately at jokes and amusing incidents. Although naturally right handed she quickly learned to use her left hand skilfully and began rejecting offers of help. She was acutely aware of her physical disability, and physiotherapy became and remained very important to her. She co-operated fully with the physiotherapist and made a tremendous effort to do everything asked of her. While Rachel was at the Rehabilitation Centre a neurologist included her in a demonstration for students and afterwards the physiotherapist observed that Rachel had co-operated willingly, followed instructions precisely and did not 'speak' at all.

Over time, recognisable words became rare. Nevertheless there can be no doubt whatever that the few real words that Rachel used in those first melancholy weeks were invaluable in providing clues to her ability to think, her understanding and her profound anxiety.

A very important decision

As soon as Rachel moved to the Rehabilitation Centre we began discussing long term plans, since it was clear that she would be unable to return to her own flat. Even if doorways were enlarged and all available aids were provided, there were too many steps, the flat was too small and, crucially, it was in the wrong place.

In the early days, we were reluctant to consider immediate transfer to a nursing home. Instead we thought about seeking a more suitable flat which could be easily visited by friends. However, as the weeks went by the permanent and profound nature of her disabilities became obvious. So the search began for a suitable nursing home.

The search was not easy and excellent homes with attractive gardens were rejected because they were too far away. We were convinced that we must find a home where Rachel would not be isolated from her friends and the activities she had valued before the stroke. And we considered it equally important for us to limit the time we spent travelling to visit Rachel, if we were to visit her frequently and maintain our other interests. We were delighted, therefore, when a friend suggested a nursing home in a very convenient position. Rachel had been in the Rehabilitation Centre for nine weeks when we visited the home.

Consulting a person with jargon aphasia about a serious decision, like moving into a nursing home, is challenging. We went through a number of steps. We discussed the obstacles Rachel would face in her own flat, such as the steps and the possible isolation from her friends. Rachel seemed to acknoweldge these difficulties and even showed signs of relief that they were being recognised. The Manager of the nursing home visited Rachel in hospital, with literature about the home. Rachel studied the brochure with interest and commented 'Hotel', which indicated that she had grasped the essential difference between a large ward in a hospital and a private room with a bathroom! We also suggested that Rachel should move into the home on a trial basis, with the option to leave if things did not work out. In fact, the move was successful. Apart from the bed, all the furniture in Rachel's room was her own and she had her own curtains, bed cover, books and pictures. It was a small but secure world which she quickly came to regard as home.

The positive aspects of Rachel living in a nursing home were immense. All aspects of her physical care became the responsibility of the home, where the staff were on duty night and day. The doctor visited regularly and qualified nursing sisters provided skilled supervision. Physiotherapy was available daily and because the physiotherapists continued the excellent work started at the Rehabilitation Centre Rachel gradually learned to walk, and as her mobility increased, so did her independence and self confidence. The routine was predictable; the environment tolerant and kind. But perhaps the greatest advantage of the nursing home was that it freed us from the responsibility of looking after Rachel's practical needs. In this way, it enabled us to remain friends, rather than 'carers'.

Caring for Rachel

If one is to survive as a person after an experience as traumatic as paralysis and the loss of speech, it is essential to retain one's self-respect and a sense of identity. This is not easy when depending upon others for many aspects of physical care including most bodily functions. Rachel accepted this situation realistically, although even before leaving hospital she insisted upon feeding herself and in many small ways demonstrated that she wanted to do things herself.

Since Rachel's stroke we have met and worked with a succession of Care Assistants. We learned to appreciate the patience, good humour and diligence of the many; to sympathise with those who found Rachel's speech not only incomprehensible but bewildering and, just occasionally, we were troubled by the impatience and hectoring attitude of the few.

Trevor Jones, who was paralysed following a skiing accident, admits that he found great difficulty in coming to terms with the need for full-time care. He describes Tanya, the best Care Assistant he ever had, as someone who was happy all the time and who could lift his spirits. Tanya was able to adapt to his moods, she was sensitive to his needs but did not fuss or draw attention to his disabilities in front of others. And, after describing the departure

of an unusually incompetent Care Assistant he says that 'he sounds like the carer from hell, but when he left I missed him because he was amusing, intelligent and good company'.*

Although Rachel accepted the fact that she depended on others for almost everything, her irritation with what she regarded as unnecessary fussing and her evident anger when she was patronised or spoken to as a child made it abundantly clear that she never became resigned to her situation. Because her speech was incomprehensible it was inevitable that most of her requests and comments were misunderstood or ignored thus increasing her frustration. Care Assistants who resented her 'commands', who were brusque and showed their own irritation were as unhappy dealing with Rachel as she was with them. Those who were able to laugh with her, distract her, amuse her or gently tease her were loved and appreciated.

To be totally dependant on others is humiliating. Consequently even small gains in independence and in mobility are highly prized. Care Assistants, friends and visitors frequently failed to appreciate how significant these small achievements were for Rachel and how important it was for her to maintain the little independence she had gained. Obviously it was often quicker and easier to do things for her rather than let her manage on her own, but accepting help because she knew that she could not cope without it was quite different from welcoming assistance with all activities twenty four hours a day. We were often aware of Rachel's barely

* Trevor Jones: *Walking on Air*, Heinemann (1997).

suppressed anger when well-meaning Care Assistants or visitors insisted on helping when help was neither wanted nor needed. Because her verbal communication was restricted to an emphatic 'No!' it was only too easy to misinterpret her brusque rejection of help as rudeness.

When away from the nursing home Rachel liked to sketch and paint in the garden. Her pencils and painting materials were left on a table and when she wanted to use them she manoeuvred her wheelchair into position. Like most people who use wheelchairs Rachel became very skilful at placing her chair exactly where she wanted it. One afternoon while Rachel was moving her wheelchair into position, Keith came along and assuming that Rachel needed help, he took hold of the handles and pushed the chair. Rachel over-reacted saying 'No No!' loudly and firmly. Keith was annoyed and departed muttering to himself about Rachel's unattractive behaviour.

Meal times provided many opportunities for misunderstanding. As Rachel was unable to use a knife she occasionally needed help when cutting meat but otherwise she became completely independent at table. However, she was often besieged by offers of help from well-intentioned fellow guests. Rachel almost always rejected these offers: sometimes she was irritated and sometimes she was amused. Sometimes her fellow guests, like Keith, were annoyed and showed it and sometimes they treated her like a badly brought up child and chastised her accordingly. But all overlooked the tremendous effort needed for Rachel to attain such independence as she had and the justified pride she felt when proving that she could do so many little things without assistance.

The significance of small gains in independence is beautifully illustrated by Trevor Jones. This man who had flown helicopters in the South Atlantic during the Falklands war eventually acquired an electric wheelchair and so was able to move around the hospital and go from one floor to the other because he learned to push the lift button. He describes the simple action of pressing the button as giving him a 'unique feeling of empowerment'.*

We soon learned that it was essential to let Rachel do by herself anything that she could do and if in doubt it was wise to ask, 'Do you need help?'. Although we could rarely understand her replies, her tone of voice and her gestures indicated clearly whether or not help was welcome.

We never regretted delegating Rachel's physical care to professional carers because only by so doing could we find time to provide her with activities that genuinely interested her, with intelligent conversation and amusement.

---

* Trevor Jones, *ibid*.

'I'm sorry, I don't understand you':
Rachel's Communication Skills and Difficulties

Speech

In the very early days after her stroke, Rachel produced nothing but a monotone babble. In some ways, this was not like speech at all. It was not obviously addressed to anyone, and did not seem to carry any meaning. Strikingly, Rachel had lost the rules about conversation, allowing her visitors virtually no opportunity to break into the continuous stream of her speech.

Gradually, a more typical form of jargon appeared. This was still, largely, incomprehensible, being strings of nonsense words. However, now there were important clues to Rachel's meaning. First of all, her speech regained its normal rhythms and intonation. This made it possible to distinguish questions from comments, and complaints from requests. Intonation was also a powerful medium for communicating her feelings. In the following incident, it was Rachel's tone which conveyed her annoyance with her friend:

> One month after the stroke Rachel wanted to move from the wheelchair to her armchair. Nursing staff were unavailable. Rachel cried hysterically and ticked me off, in jargon, for not helping her. Eventually a nurse was persuaded to lift Rachel into her chair. When settled, Rachel looked at me and said: 'you see'.

This incident illustrates another feature of Rachel's speech at this time, namely the presence of the occasional real word. These real words provided the first clues that Rachel's personality and humour were still very much intact.

> Soon after the stroke Rachel was eating lunch in her geriatric ward in hospital. She lifted her glass of water and said 'cheers to the old dears'.
>
> Two months later I returned from Paris with a charming ceramic bowl made by a friend. Rachel held it professionally in her left hand and said 'very nice'. She seemed happy to continue holding and looking at it.
>
> On another occasion, I was sitting by Rachel's bed, correcting the last article she had written before her stroke. Her other visitor did not notice the papers on the table and moved them. Rachel immediately pulled them back and said 'How dare you'.

Some individuals with jargon aphasia produce more and more real words at time progresses, so much so, that the original neologisms, or nonsense words, disappear. Unfortunately, this was not the case with Rachel. Instead, her speech remained primarily neologistic.

Understanding

Understanding of speech is often very impaired in jargon aphasia. In some cases the problem is so severe that it seems that everyone is talking in a foreign language.

Formal comprehension tests, administered by the speech and language therapists, suggested that Rachel's understanding of speech was poor, at least in the early days after her stroke. However, on the ward, there were hints that Rachel was comprehending quite a lot of what was said to her:

Rachel's visitors were talking about the South of France. Rachel was taking part in the conversation, using her jargon. However, the occasional real word, such as 'Mediterranean', suggested that she had at least grasped the topic.

Two months after the stroke Rachel was drinking her coffee on the ward. Someone said: 'you'll need a cigar with that'. Rachel immediately mimed smoking a cigar and laughed.

At about 4pm Rachel began crying inconsolably. There was anger as well as tears and a worrying degree of distress. This continued for about two hours, during which time she used an entire box of tissues. Then in the middle of the fury and jargon one word 'home' emerged. I decided to talk about home. I discussed all the reasons why she couldn't go straight home, listing the practical problems such as the bathroom, the steps and the need for more time. Rachel became very calm and reasonable. She listened, thought and agreed. Finally, she held my hand two or three times and said 'thank you'.

Rachel's grasp of situations and social meaning was never disrupted by her stroke. She could pick up hints about what people were feeling, could interpret events and make inferences from them. This is beautifully illustrated in the following story:

> On arriving at the nursing home, Rachel was placed next to Betty in the dining room. Betty was severely physically disabled but she had a gentle manner and a quiet voice. At meal times, Rachel often spoke to Betty, assuming that she understood. Betty would give a non-committal reply such as 'of course' or 'is that so?'.
>
> Betty spent much of her time in the day-room, which was next to her bedroom at the far end of the building. Once Rachel had learnt to walk again, she visited Betty every day. She would sit down beside her, talk to her for five or ten minutes and then walk back to her own room. Betty always showed interest in Rachel's 'conversation', answering 'is that so?' or 'really' from time to time. It was clear that Rachel had become very fond of Betty and on Betty's birthday Rachel stood in front of her wheelchair, presented her with some flowers, and made what was obviously intended to be a gracious speech.
>
> Some months later when Rachel returned from holiday she walked towards the day room to see Betty. As she passed her bedroom, she saw Betty lying in bed obviously very ill. The next day Rachel walked again to the day room. This time Betty's bedroom door was shut and her name removed from the name plate on the door. Rachel looked at the name plate, 'commented', turned around and walked back to her own room. She never visited that day room again.

About a year after her stroke, it became possible to assess Rachel's comprehension more fully. Now a more promising picture emerged. She could easily carry out single word tasks, like matching a spoken word to a picture. She could respond equally well to sentences. For example, in one task we told Rachel that she was going to hear some sentences, some of which contained a nonsense word, e.g. *The famous star visited the cottee patients.*

Rachel had to indicate which sentences were correct and which were not, by pointing to a tick or cross. This she could do with relative ease, despite the rather bizarre nature of the task. We could therefore conclude that, when listening to other people, she could distinguish real from nonsense words, even if those words appeared in sentences.

Why was there such a discrepancy between Rachel's early comprehension tests and the evidence of her friends? Of course, in normal conversation, there are many props to understanding. People may point to what they mean, use pictures or exaggerate their tone of voice. Rachel was talking to friends. She knew their interests and concerns so could guess their likely topic of conversation. None of these clues are available in testing. However, this may not be the whole story. We must also accept that testing may underestimate people's comprehension abilities. In a test, the person has to not only understand a word, or phrase, but also act upon that understanding, ie by pointing to a picture. In Rachel's case, it may have been these demands which caused the problem.

Writing

There was a huge gulf between Rachel's speech and writing. Speech was fluent, even non-stop, whereas writing was extremely hesitant. Rachel was apparently oblivious to her speech errors, but noticed and tried to correct her writing errors. Furthermore, even in the early days after her stroke, some writing skills were observed:

> After two weeks at the rehabilitation centre I put some paper on her table and a pen in her hand and suggested that she should write. At first she was very reluctant to do so but eventually she scribbled along the line, very carefully, from right to left. The result obviously annoyed her and she put the pen down. During the following few weeks Rachel learned to write from left to right and began using letters and writing single 'words', although letters were often in the wrong order or omitted altogether. For instance, she wrote 'b..nk' and then said 'bank'. This led to a discussion about money and how her finances were being managed. On another occasion, Rachel drew a very good picture of a teddy bear to amuse her brother, and wrote BEABR beneath it. She immediately spotted that this was not quite right, and crossed out the second B.
>
> I tried using scrabble tiles with Rachel. I placed the jumbled letters of Rachel's name in front of her. Without hesitation, Rachel reorganised them correctly. She soon became very persistent in practising writing her name, rejecting help and achieving success within two weeks. Through constant practice her hand writing improved considerably although it never became fluent.

These emerging writing skills became crucial in Rachel's later therapy (see following section).

Reading

It was very difficult to judge Rachel's comprehension of what she read. Any attempt to read aloud simply resulted in jargon. However, there were hints of some preserved abilities:

> Evidence that Rachel could read accumulated slowly. When a newspaper was left on a table beside her, she picked it up, turned it up the right way and appeared to read it. Her response to letters varied; when signatures were familiar, she would point to them and say 'ah' as if in recognition. Once she received a card with about twelve signatures and she ran her finger down the list, occasionally stopping and commenting. Although she was often seen reading journals and studying catalogues and magazines, there was no way of knowing how much she understood. However, she marked passages intelligently, frequently pointing out items which interested her. One day when reading an article in French, she pointed to a passage containing a difficult phrase, and was relieved when the meaning was explained.
>
> Three months after the stroke Rachel was shown the programme of a conference being held at the Freer Gallery in Washington. I chatted about the event and talked about the different speakers. Whenever the speakers were mentioned, Rachel pointed to their names written in the programme.
>
> On another occasion Rachel was delighted with an illustration on the cover of a catalogue which she pointed at with enthusiasm. She then turned to page eight in the catalogue where she had marked the text relating to the cover illustration.

Reading comprehension can be formally assessed. For example, we can ask people to match a written word to a picture or sort written words into appropriate categories. Tasks like these were given to Rachel about a year after her stroke and they confirmed that she could indeed understand written words. However, she did make mistakes and, interestingly, her comprehension of writing seemed poorer than her comprehension of speech.

However, there is more to reading than just understanding single words or sentences. What we read is an aspect of who we are. Although Rachel's reading was not perfect it was clearly a vital activity for her. Both before and after her stroke she was a highly literary person:

> Confronted with the severity of Rachel's speech and communication problems friends and acquaintances must have wondered whether there was any point in sending her cards and letters. However as Rachel was accustomed to receiving professional and personal mail, we thought it essential for post to appear regularly. For Rachel professional information formed a significant part of her previous life and we felt sure that in order to sustain her self-respect and identity in the future, it was essential to keep up the flow of newsletters, reports, notices and journals. In addition, they would provide a useful source for work with speech and language therapists.
>
> At first Rachel appeared to take little interest in her correspondence but its importance increased steadily. We observed that any form of communication such as reading, talking or listening was very demanding and consequently very tiring. Initially, Rachel rejected long letters altogether, however interesting or

entertaining the content. This could have been because the mental effort needed to cope with a complicated story was out of proportion to the information gained. On the other hand, attractive cards or postcards with a few cheerful words, were prized. Familiar writing and, most importantly, familiar signatures were studied and valued.

We know from research that people with aphasia may undertake a range of reading activities which are apparently beyond their capabilities. It could be that our testing underestimates their skills. Alternatively, or in addition, aphasic people may benefit from the support of family and friends. In other words, activities which were formerly done independently, are now done in collaboration with others. This was certainly the case for Rachel:

> Although Rachel insisted on reading all cards and letters herself, we suspected that she found some handwriting difficult to read. For this reason we always asked to see cards and other correspondence. We then discussed the people, places and the information in conversation with her.
>
> Letters referring to several people by name presented a serious problem for Rachel, as she had great difficulty with names. On the other hand, when shown a photograph she would recognise the person immediately. Frequently, we had to place the people referred to in context by talking about their activities, or describing their appearance. Not all of Rachel's correspondents were known to us. For this reason we asked the staff of her nursing home to retain the envelopes if they opened her post, as the senders may have given their full name and address on the outside.

Self-Monitoring

People with jargon aphasia are often unaware of their speech difficulties. This was certainly the case for Rachel. Recordings of her speech showed no signs that she was trying to correct her output. For example, she did not obviously struggle to find words and there were very few hesitations. Her friends also observed this lack of awareness:

> Rachel seemed to have no idea that her speech was not making sense. She conversed with friends just as she always had, laughing at jokes and apparently reciprocating with her own stories. When not understood she was indignant.

Rachel's lack of awareness made speech and language therapy very difficult, as she could not see why intervention was needed. She was similarly resistant when alternative forms of communication were suggested:

> While still at the rehabilitation centre Rachel was having difficulty explaining when she needed the lavatory, which caused discomfort and the occasional accident. The speech and language therapist tried to encourage her to use a picture to communicate when she needed to go to the lavatory. Rachel was furious at the suggestion and turned the picture face down on her table. She found the idea undignified and could not see why a picture was needed when she could simply tell staff.

It is very difficult to understand why Rachel could not 'hear' her own speech, especially as she could clearly hear and understand the speech of others. Her lack of awareness was also very selective. For example, she fully appreciated her physical difficulties and participated very willingly in physiotherapy. She also recognised her writing problems.

Rachel's oblivion to her speech problems persisted, even when she was explicitly told that she was not making sense. For example, her speech and language therapist tried to inhibit her jargon by telling her to stop talking and by using a 'sh' gesture. Despite this, Rachel carried on talking as before. Friends were also honest with her:

> From the outset we adopted a flexible approach to Rachel's jargon. If Rachel was trying to tell us something, or ask a question we were always honest with her about whether or not we understood, often saying 'I'm sorry I don't understand you'. This we decided was not appropriate if Rachel was tearful or frustrated. On these occasions we would attempt to calm her down first, and then try to resolve the problem.

Much later after her stroke, Rachel showed a few signs of self-awareness and with this, came an increase in her frustration:

> On one occasion, I arrived to find Rachel in evident distress. Something had happened with one of the care staff. Rachel struggled to explain the problem. Unusually, her speech was very hesitant, with long pauses and searching for words: 'she was ... she ... she did'. Eventually, Rachel realised that she was not getting her message across and waved her hand in sad resignation.

These moments of self-realisation were rare. It seemed that Rachel was the one person who was not privy to the severity of her speech problem.

Non-verbal Communication Skills

Many people with aphasia supplement formal language with non-verbal communication, such as gesture and drawing. In some cases such skills seem untouched by the aphasia, in which case the person may turn to them spontaneously. In other cases, even these apparently non-linguistic modalities can be impaired. For example, gestures may be difficult to execute and even if the person can draw quite well, they may not think to use drawing to convey information. For this reason, non-verbal communication skills are often a focus for therapy.

People with aphasia can become very skilled users of non-verbal communication. For example, this illustration shows a sketch drawn by an aphasic man to convey his former work as a tugboat skipper.

Another man, who had no speech, became particularly adept at using songs. For example, wanting to communicate that he had been to a wedding over the weekend, he sang the tune of 'Daisy Daisy' and to convey that he had been on holiday: 'Oh, I do like to be beside the Seaside'.

Rachel seemed less willing to employ such techniques, at least in the early stages:

> As Rachel could not make herself understood verbally it was obvious that she should be persuaded to use gestures. Within weeks of her stroke she was encouraged to do this but, probably because she was convinced that her speech could be understood, she resisted all our efforts. Furthermore, she refused to co-operate by pointing to pictures, however carefully selected and presented. These she brushed aside in disdain or indignation.
>
> It was a year or more before she began to use gestures spontaneously and another year before she did so effectively. No doubt a growing acceptance that she was often failing to make herself understood drove her to use gestures for practical purposes. Then she would point to the remains of a tube of toothpaste or an empty soap dish to indicate that she needed a replacement. On one occasion, I arrived in Rachel's room to find her clearly very agitated. She immediately pointed to her bed and complained about something in an indignant voice. On investigation, it emerged that one of the pillows was without a pillow case. Even after this was put right by the care assistant, Rachel continued to point to the bed and complain in an indignant tone of voice. I therefore investigated further. Sure enough Rachel was right. There was no bottom sheet.

With the use of gestures, such as pointing, came a willingness to use objects in the environment to convey information. The following incident illustrates this:

> One day Rachel was obviously upset and annoyed about something but there was nothing in her agitated 'conversation' to indicate what was troubling her. I said that I was sorry, that I knew that she was very concerned about something but I could not understand her. Rachel paused, stood up and going over to her bookcase she took a photograph album from the shelf and went through it until she came to a picture of herself in a red and white striped shirt. Then she handed me the album and prodded the shirt with her forefinger. 'Oh' I said 'Have you lost your shirt?' Rachel looked relieved, closed the album and 'commented' in an exasperated voice which I interpreted as 'I've been telling you that for the last fifteen minutes. Will you please find it'.

This incident not only illustrates Rachel's skills in using the objects in her environment, it is also an excellent example of how intelligence is intact in aphasia. Not only did Rachel remember the relevant photograph she could also see its potential for solving the problem at hand.

Communicating Emotion

Rachel's use of non-verbal modalities partly depended on the type of information that was being conveyed. Although she made limited use of such techniques to convey specific needs or facts, they were used very extensively to convey feelings:

> From the time that Rachel was in the rehabilitation centre she used gestures, facial expressions and exclamations to express her opinions and views. While still at the centre a friend visited Rachel bringing with her twelve photographs of antiques she thought would be of interest. Rachel was delighted. She looked carefully at each one, 'commenting' from time to time with enthusiasm but putting one aside with an expression of disgust. She had never liked that type of object.

It was also striking that Rachel's occasional real words tended to be highly emotional. For example, she dismissed the Nursing Home Christmas activities as 'horrible', and was able to bellow 'get out' at the nursing home cat who wandered into her room uninvited.*

Although Rachel could convey her feelings, identifying the source of these feelings was much more problematic:

> We often realised that Rachel was seeking help, information or rassurance, but it was rarely possible to grasp what was troubling her. Sometimes Rachel pointed to the corridor outside her room when 'talking' about something that had upset her, so one assumed that there had been a problem with another resident, with a care assistant or perhaps there had been a difficult situation in the dining room, but there was no way of knowing.

---

* As far back as 1870, Hughlings Jackson observed that aphasic people are often better at communicating emotion than they are at communicating statements or facts. This may be because such communication calls upon very automatic, reflexive systems and therefore depends less upon formal language abilities.

Choosing Speech

Although Rachel learnt to employ some diversity in her communication, her preferred mode remained speech, despite the fact that this was often incomprehensible. It is difficult to judge why she made this choice. One factor was almost certainly her poor self-monitoring, which obscured the extent of her speech problems from her. However, this may not be the whole story. To sacrifice speech is to sacrifice a part of your personality. Perhaps Rachel opted for jargon rather than silence because in this way she felt more true to herself.

Making Progress
Therapy with Rachel

Survivors of stroke often acquire lasting disabilities. Like many others, Rachel was faced with a paralysis of one side of her body, in her case the right, together with a profound speech and language problem. Although rarely eliminated, such disabilities can be reduced through therapy. Therapy can also help people to compensate for their problems, by making use of alternative strategies and techniques.

Rachel had three kinds of therapy after her stroke. The physiotherapists worked on balance, walking, climbing steps and using her right arm. Occupational therapists advised on mobility aids, like her wheelchair; and speech and language therapists tried to improve her communication.

The amount of therapy received after stroke varies a great deal. Some people continue with therapy for a year, or even longer, while others are discharged after just a few sessions. Such inequalities are worrying and many stroke survivors feel that they are not given enough therapy support.

Rachel received quite extensive therapy after her stroke, although from various sources. Her case was unusual in that she was involved in a university based research programme, which intensified her speech and language therapy. However, it should also be stressed that she received considerable input from both hospital and community based NHS therapists.

This section will focus mainly on the content of Rachel's speech and language therapy, and on her response to that therapy. We will also give a brief account of her physiotherapy.

Speech and Language Therapy for Aphasia

In many ways, aphasia therapy is still in its infancy. One reason for this is the sheer diversity of problems seen in aphasia. Just as all aphasic people are different, so therapy for their problems has to be different. We cannot simply develop one therapy which is served up to everyone.

Despite this, there are some common themes in aphasia therapy. For example, we have begun to identify approaches which can help with word finding problems and others which improve reading or sentence comprehension. Furthermore, research has shown that these approaches can bring about small, but measurable improvements, at least in the individuals studied.

Not all aphasia therapy aims directly to improve language skills. Another important aspect helps the person to compensate for their problems. For example, if someone can neither speak or write, it is sensible to encourage them to use gestures or drawings.

People with jargon aphasia present a serious challenge to the speech and language therapist, partly because their problems are so severe. Additionally, the lack of self-monitoring makes it difficult for the person to see that therapy is needed in the first place. Even if the person does accept therapy, the problems of jargon are very difficult to treat. We are still unsure about how to help the person monitor their speech better, let alone change it. For this reason, a lot of therapists would advocate the use of compensatory therapies. This was very much the approach taken with Rachel.

Speech and Language Therapy in the Early Days

Like many jargon speakers, Rachel found it very difficult to participate in speech and language therapy in the first few weeks after her stroke. Sessions were tiring and frustrating, with little evidence of progress:

> I observed Rachel in a long therapy session, most of which was spent classifying pictures and words. Rachel coped well at first. As the difficulty increased she started to fail and became tearful. She was also exhausted and once she returned to the ward fell fast asleep.

At this time, Rachel was producing an almost continual stream of jargon. It was important to try to reduce this, at least so that she could listen to other people. However, suppressing the jargon was very difficult:

> We were advised to 'stop Rachel talking'. The speech

and language therapist even suggested putting a finger over the lips in a 'shush' gesture. In practice, this advice was very difficult to follow. The line between persuading Rachel to stop talking and upsetting her was a fine one. We felt we were undermining her confidence and attempts to quieten her resulted in anger and distress, particularly when she was tired.

The other problem was that not all her speech was meaningless. Simply stopping Rachel from talking would eliminate important snippets of communication:

> Rachel was visited by a very sensible curate. He had previously been a nurse and so understood Rachel's situation. After the visit Rachel commented approvingly 'good man'. She then lapsed into jargon, obviously trying to tell us something important. Of course, we could not understand. Then, in the midst of the confusion, a real phrase emerged: 'something I meant to tell you ... parish'. It suddenly became clear that she was worrying about her church responsibilities and we were able to explain to her what had been done about these. Although troubled at first, Rachel was gradually reassured.

For Rachel's friends, inhibiting speech was not a practical or even a desirable aim (although this may be productive with other people).

Speech was clearly not changing in the early stages. However, there were signs that Rachel might be able to use alternative modes of communication. For example, she was making attempts to write her name and to arrange words with scrabble tiles. Although not hopeful about speech, Rachel's friends felt that this might be a productive avenue for therapy:

> About three months after Rachel's stroke I wrote the following extract in my diary: 'Speech therapy, as such, will not help Rachel to talk coherently, of that I am convinced'. It became clear to us that we would have to develop non-verbal forms of communication. However, we also realised that this would be difficult for Rachel.

Alternatives to Speech — Later Speech and Language Therapy*

We first met Rachel eighteen months after her stroke, when she joined our Medical Research Council project. Like her friends, we were not optimistic about being able to change Rachel's speech. However, there were signs of subtle writing abilities, which possibly could be improved in therapy. For example, we noted Rachel's ability to arrange scrabble tiles into words. We also detected some copying abilities. In one test, we showed Rachel a written word for about fifteen seconds. We then covered the word up and asked her to copy it from memory. Rachel could do this quite well, which showed that she had some ideas about how words should be written. There was one last important sign. As far as we could tell, Rachel was oblivious to her jargon. She certainly made no obvious attempt to correct her speech. In contrast, she was very

---

* Much of the speech and language therapy described in this section was developed and administered in collaboration with Sarah Morrison, St John's Therapy Centre, Wandsworth Community Health Trust.

aware of her writing problems. She was critical of her attempts to write words and would accept corrections supplied by the therapist. Importantly, Rachel was willing to work on writing, which was not the case for her speech. Indeed, her friends were already giving Rachel informal writing tasks, like copying words into sentences.

We decided that therapy should aim to give Rachel some basic writing skills. It is important to be explicit about what we were hoping to achieve. Rachel had been a very sophisticated writer before her stroke, with an impressive list of publications. We were not aiming to recover anything like this level of ability. Rather, we were thinking that Rachel might learn to write a *few* words. If these words were sensibly chosen they could be helpful in overcoming at least some of the break-downs in communication which punctuated her life. For example, like many Nursing Home residents, Rachel sometimes had problems with her laundry. If she could write words like 'blouse' or 'trousers' when items went missing, she might regain a little control over this aspect of her life.

Although there were signs that writing might be productive, at this time Rachel was not able to write any words unaided. The first step in therapy, therefore, was to help her to write a small set of useful words. We restricted the number to about thirty, as we felt that Rachel would not be able to learn any more at one time.

Our first problem was choosing the words. Here her friends helped by providing vocabulary which they thought would be useful. This vocabulary included words to do with food, clothing, places that Rachel visited and terms associated with her art interests. We spent fourteen therapy sessions practising these words (each session lasted about half an hour). The sessions were frequent, i.e. three times a week, because we thought Rachel would need intensive exposure to the words in order to learn them.

How did we teach the words? The tasks were very mundane. At first, we asked Rachel to sort out each word, using letter tiles. Then we made this more difficult by providing her with the letters of two words, which had to be separated and sorted. Once she had arranged a word, we asked her to copy it. At a later stage, this was made more demanding by covering up the word before she wrote it down. Finally, we showed Rachel pictures of the items and asked her to write their names. Here she was initially given the first letter as a clue, then she had to remember the whole word on her own. You can see from this description that Rachel's therapy involved a few familiar and repeated tasks, which gradually increased in difficulty. This is typical of much speech and language therapy.

At the beginning of this therapy period Rachel could write none of the words, even when we cued her with the first letter. After therapy, she could write twelve on her own and a further eleven following a first letter cue. Although encouraging, these gains were quite limited. Rachel could still only write a very small number of words, and, rather depressingly, she was not using her writing to help her communicate in every day life. So, even though she had learnt the word 'soap' she did not use it to ask friends to buy her more soap when hers had run out.

The first therapy programme did prove one thing. Clearly Rachel could take part in therapy and learn new skills, despite her very severe problems. We therefore pressed on. We decided that we needed to do two things: we needed to increase the number of words that Rachel could write and we needed to encourage Rachel to use her writing when communicating with other people. The first aim was straight forward. We simply chose another set of words (again with her friends' help), and practised them using exactly the same tasks as in the first therapy programme. Encouragingly, Rachel learnt these new words well. Indeed, she acquired more words in this second programme, and learnt them slightly more quickly.

The second aim required tasks which would encourage Rachel to use writing to convey information. For example, we might show her a picture and ask her to communicate its contents to a friend, by writing its name. In another task, we drew a map of Rachel's local area and asked her to show us where she had been using her writing. Similarly, we would ask questions about any visits she had made. For example, we might ask 'where did you go on Thursday?' and she would write 'restaurant'.

This therapy also brought about improvements. We evaluated it by asking Rachel a series of questions before and after therapy, which could be answered using treated words. For example, we might ask 'Where did you go on holiday?' for the target word 'France'. Before therapy, Rachel could only answer four of the questions. After therapy, she succeeded with twenty one. It seemed that Rachel could now use her writing slightly more flexibly. However, and it was a big however, Rachel was still not using writing outside therapy sessions.

What was stopping Rachel from writing? The problem we encountered occurs in many forms of therapy (not just speech and language therapy), in that people often learn skills in one setting which do not generalise to another. In Rachel's case there was a further factor. Rachel was still, apparently, unaware of her speech problems. She could not therefore appreciate the need for writing. As far as she was concerned, she could simply tell people what she wanted. We wondered if there was a third problem. It might be that Rachel could not see how she could translate the complex messages which she wished to convey into the single words which she could now write.

Our third period of therapy tried to tackle this problem. We were very blunt with Rachel. We explained that people often could not understand what she was saying and that, instead, she might write things down. Of course, this approach is risky. It is hurtful to be told that your speech makes no sense, and hard to grasp if you yourself cannot see the problem. We therefore risked losing Rachel's trust. For this reason, it is probably best to employ such techniques after a working relationship has been established with the aphasic person. It is also important to offer something positive instead of speech — in this case writing.

The second dimension of therapy tried to show

Rachel how she could use single words to give people clues about what she wanted to say. This therapy involved pairing messages with single words. For example, in one task we gave Rachel two written messages:

'The laundry is late this week.'
'My blouse needs to be washed.'

She was then given a choice of three words (shirt, vicar, park) and asked to indicate which one was associated with the messages. The task was then made more difficult by just giving Rachel a message and asking her to write down an associated word. For example:

'Supposing you wanted to say that you have been to the Poussin exhibition. What could you write?' (she should write 'gallery').

Rachel showed further signs of progress after this period of therapy. Once again, she learnt some new words. More importantly, she was able to write these words to convey given messages. Finally, there were hints that Rachel was beginning to use writing in her daily life. For instance she wrote 'trou' to indicate that her trousers had not been returned from the laundry. She was able to communicate who had brought her flowers by writing the person's name and, on another occasion, wrote a close enough approximation of some friend's names to convey that she was still waiting to see them.

What did speech and language therapy achieve with Rachel? At the start, she could not write anything spontaneously. Therapy helped her to acquire a small set of useful, everyday words. In addition, Rachel could attempt to write words which were not practised in therapy. Although these might not be completely accurate, they were often close enough for us to guess the target. Rachel found it harder to use her writing communicatively. The latter stages of therapy attempted to address this problem. At the end of this therapy Rachel would, occasionally, turn to writing when communication broke down.

There were many things that therapy did not achieve. Rachel's speech was completely unchanged and communicating with her was still extremely difficult. She remained largely unaware of her speech problems. Although progress was made in writing it was woefully limited. Above all, Rachel still lacked a medium which could carry the broad sweep of her thoughts and ideas. Yet now, she could take her diary, find the right date and write in the name of her therapist to mark the next appointment. For Rachel, this was not a trivial gain.

There was no need to talk — The importance of physiotherapy for Rachel

It would be impossible to tell Rachel's story without including a comment on her response to physiotherapy. As soon as she was admitted to the Rehabilitation Centre physiotherapy sessions began and from the outset she displayed enormous determination in her effort to regain mobility and the use of her right hand. Although often tearful and tired her tenacity was impressive and that, together with the professional skills of the physiotherapist, who handled her with patience and optimism, gradually achieved results.

At the nursing home appropriate physiotherapy continued daily and when we took Rachel away for holidays another excellent physiotherapist took over. To all these physiotherapists Rachel responded with enthusiasm. Communication was never a problem as she understood their instructions and followed them carefully. There was no need for her to talk and consequently no misunderstanding and no frustration. The physiotherapists responded to her exclamations of pain or pleasure with firmness, amusement and endless encouragement ensuring that the sessions were joyful occasions despite the tears and the enormous effort involved.

There can be no doubt that Rachel's progress, although very slow, was a continual source of reassurance and an important factor in restoring her confidence and self-respect. Furthermore, each small step increased the opportunities for her to develop independence and to join in social activities. We recall with pleasure the first time Rachel stood upright in the Rehabilitation Centre gym, albeit in a frame with a great deal of support. This was an event of real excitement for all of us. Later she learned to propel herself about in her wheelchair so that she could go in to the dining room by herself, explore other rooms and corridors and find people to talk to. Then when she could walk alone with the aid of a tripod we noticed that she often had brief 'conversations' with the receptionist at the nursing home and cheery exchanges with care staff, cooks and cleaners as she walked along the corridors. And one day when she was staying away from the nursing home she surprised us by walking through the house to a room where she heard voices. She stood in the doorway laughing, as if to say, 'you didn't think I could do this, did you?'. Eventually she learned to walk up and down stairs. This was a major triumph as it enabled her to visit friends, hotels, restaurants and exhibitions without undue difficulty. Thus her anxiety decreased, her confidence increased and her whole world expanded.

'What do you do when she laughs?' Friends, visitors and staff

The communication problems generated by jargon aphasia are not only felt by the aphasic person. They are also felt by everyone in contact with that person. Conversing with a jargon speaker is difficult and disconcerting. It is nigh on impossible to understand their speech, and when you talk, it is hard to judge how much has been understood. In the midst of all this confusion, the person with jargon aphasia is apparently oblivious of the problem, or even quite annoyed with their friend for failing to get the message.

Despite these difficulties, some of the communication problems generated by jargon aphasia can be helped by very simple advice. This was often the case with Rachel's care staff:

> Sandra came into Rachel's room holding the menu. Standing just in front of Rachel she asked: 'What will you have for lunch? Fried fish or chicken casserole?'. Rachel replied in jargon and, of course, Sandra couldn't understand her. So she repeated the question, this time shouting: 'What would you like for lunch?, fried fish or casserole?' Rachel winced, moving her head to one side as if trying to escape the noise. I

intervened. 'Give Rachel the menu and ask her to point to what she wants. You could read it to her quietly'. Muttering sceptically:'if you think it would help', Sandra followed these instructions. Immediately Rachel pointed to her choice, looked pleased and all was well.

We often provided this kind of advice to people in contact with Rachel. Typical tips included:

Remember that Rachel is neither deaf nor confused

Speak clearly but in a normal way

Keep speech simple, and avoid long complicated messages.

It can help to repeat questions slowly and to add some gestures.

Do not raise issues which cannot be resolved, this can bring distress.

Use props, such as picture books and photo albums.

Talk about topics that interest Rachel, such as art.

Successful care staff followed these tips. Harriet was a typical example:

Harriet was one of Rachel's favourites. She spotted Rachel's sense of humour and often made her laugh, perhaps with a funny tone of voice, or through self mockery. Her speech was slow and clear without being patronising. She was also careful to learn Rachel's routine, and to work within it. If Rachel made a stand on some issue, even if it seemed irrational, Harriet went along with it. On one occasion Rachel's nails needed cutting. Yet, when Harriet tried to cut them, Rachel objected. It would have been very difficult to find out the reason for this objection. So, sensibly, Harriet didn't try. Instead, she simply stopped. When she returned to the issue later, Rachel happily consented.

Despite the communication difficulties, Rachel got on well with most of the care staff. She accepted the need for help in a perfectly matter of fact way. Any disagreements usually occured because Rachel felt that she was being patronised:

> A new care assistant asked Rachel a question, to which she responded in jargon. I said quietly, 'Rachel can understand you, but you will not understand her'. Rachel made a further 'comment', whereupon the care assistant, who had obviously never encountered jargon aphasia before, roared with laughter. Rachel was furious. She slapped her hand on the table in front of her and let forth a volley of indignant jargon. The care assistant, who had not intended to cause offence, said: 'Be nice to me!' But it is difficult to be 'nice' when one is being laughed at, how ever good natured the laughter.

The challenges faced by Rachel's care staff were also faced by her visitors. Friends also had to cope with their own distress at seeing Rachel so altered. Yet, visits could be very successful:

> One afternoon, shortly after Rachel was transferred to a nursing home, she was visited by Alison. As Alison had visited Rachel in the rehabilitation unit she was aware of Rachel's speech problems and brought with her several ceramic objects to discuss during the visit. The visit went well. Rachel showed genuine interest in the objects and Alison discussed them in a sensible, professional manner, which Rachel found reassuring.
>
> Perhaps Rachel's most successful visitor was her

brother who came almost every week bringing a single flower or a piece of fruit. Always companionable, he told her about his activities and chatted about mutual friends. After trips abroad he brought his photographs and recounted his adventures. He encouraged and entertained her, without exhausting or making demands on her.

Sadly, after Rachel had lived in the nursing home for eighteen months, her brother died suddenly. When told about his death, Rachel's reaction was completely in character. She cried briefly and then pulled herself together and 'talked' about him. The manager of the nursing home, having been told the news, came to see Rachel. Rachel listened to her thoughtful and sympathetic comments. Then she picked up her diary, found the last day on which her brother had visited and pointing to his name said 'Great man!'

Unsuccessful exchanges usually arose when the visitor had not been sufficiently briefed. It was particularly vital for *new* visitors to be properly introduced and to be given guidance so that they could cope when left alone. This basic precept was not followed by a volunteer visitor, with disastrous results:

> Because of Rachel's social isolation, regular visiting was essential. It was suggested that someone from a voluntary organisation might help. This seemed a sensible idea and the organiser of visitors met Rachel with me and a speech and language therapist, in order to find out Rachel's needs.
>
> Some weeks later, a Sister in the nursing home told me that a visitor from the organisation would be coming to see Rachel that week. Knowing that a stranger might have difficulty in coping unless introduced to Rachel and shown where to find photograph albums etc, I decided to visit Rachel at the same time. However, on arriving at the reception desk, I was told

there was someone waiting to see me. There, sitting tense and trembling, was the volunteer visitor. Unfortunately, she had tried to introduce herself to Rachel without me. Obviously the visit had not gone well. Rachel had ordered the visitor out of the room and thrown her copy of Country Life after her.

Why did Rachel behave like that? At this time Rachel was rather troubled by confused fellow residents who tended to wander into her room by mistake. Rachel probably mistook the volunteer for such a resident. However, in talking to the volunteer, it became clear that even if she had gained entry, the visit was unlikely to succeed. She had no understanding of Rachel's communication problems. 'Visiting' for her meant conversation and as there could be no ordinary conversation with Rachel, the visit was doomed to failure.

How should this visit have been managed? First of all, the visitor needed to be carefully introduced to Rachel. The times of her visits should have been planned and entered into Rachel's diary. The visitor also needed training. She needed a better understanding of aphasia generally and of Rachel's jargon in particular. Above all, she needed guidance about how to communicate with Rachel. An interim period, in which she visited Rachel with one of us, would have been helpful. Such planning and preparation takes time. However, if it had been done, a successful long term contact could have been forged between Rachel and a volunteer. As it was, this unfortunate volunteer was placed in an impossible situation and the project failed at the first hurdle.

Communication is not only hampered by a lack of knowledge, it can also be impeded by false beliefs.

This is particularly so in cases of jargon aphasia, where the mysterious nature of the problem generates its own myths. One such myth is that the person is speaking in a code which might somehow be cracked. This myth was often expressed by those in contact with Rachel:

> Some time after Rachel moved to the nursing home it was suggested that she would benefit from some specialised, private, physiotherapy. The first session went well. The therapist had a sensible sympathetic manner and was able to convey her instructions to Rachel without difficulty, often without speech. Rachel made numerous 'comments' during the session, always in jargon. As often happened, her jargon sounded rather repetitive, with one word 'spatika' frequently recurring. The physio was convinced that this word carried a special meaning for Rachel and asked: 'What does spatika mean?'. Like many others, the physio thought that increasing contact with Rachel might crack the code. As Rachel was leaving, she announced confidently: 'by the end of the week I will have worked it out'.

The belief that the jargon is a code generates other false beliefs. One is that there may be individuals who are privy to the code and can therefore act as interpreters:

> Rachel was particularly upset one day and kept pointing to her chest of drawers. On investigation, it emerged that she had run out of clean shirts. I went to find one of the care staff, who fetched Rachel's clean clothes from the laundry. However, Rachel was still upset. She continued to point to the chest of drawers and her jargon became more emphatic. The care assistant turned to me and asked: 'what is she saying?'. I, of course, was none the wiser. With this, the care

assistant rushed out of the room calling to me: 'I'll go and find someone who can understand what she is saying'.

Another common myth is that the code might be cracked by some kind of machine or computer. Again, this presupposes that the jargon is systematic, which is simply not the case. Unfortunately, most people with jargon aphasia also find it difficult to use computers as communication aids, which was true for Rachel:

> Julian visited Rachel while she was at the Rehabilitation Centre. An interesting man who had devised various electronic aids for people with speech problems, he arrived prepared to help Rachel. However, having spent some time with her could not imagine how his aids could assist her. Julian never visited Rachel again, which was sad as she enjoyed his company.

The very profound communication problems can obscure what is still 'normal' in the aphasic person's social behaviour. Aphasic people enjoy social contact just as much as they ever did and appreciate social niceties. Rachel remained a highly hospitable person, offering visitors chocolates and showing an interest in their concerns. She could also follow the *tone* of a conversation, even if the precise meaning of the words eluded her. Thus, she knew when a joke had been made and could recognise if people were annoyed or upset. Sadly, these preserved skills were not always appreciated by friends.

> One visitor, after spending a rather awkward fifteen minutes in Rachel's company left saying: 'What do you

do when she laughs?'. Of course, the answer was, 'join in'. Rachel had a lively sense of humour and was readily amused by ridiculous situations and verbal anecdotes. There was rarely any doubt that we were all laughing at the same thing.

Living with Dignity after Stroke
The Long Term

One of the decisions that has to be made when a person has a stroke is whether or not they can continue living in their own home. Numerous questions have to be taken into account. Can the person manage physically? What are the safety implications? Will they have enough support? When the person lives alone these questions may be all the more pressing.

Another difficulty is enabling the person with aphasia to express their views about returning home. In so doing, it is important that the person is helped to make an *informed* judgement, ie that they understand all the implications of either returning home or living in residential care. Here the speech and language therapist can help. He or she can advise about how to ask comprehensible questions and on how to get reliable responses to those questions. When the aphasia is very severe, the only way to probe the person's feelings may be to give them the chance to experience the options and observe their response. For example, the person's attachment to their own home can be gauged through a home visit. Alternatively or additionally, they might move into a residential home for a trial period. If this proves successful, more permanent arrangements can be discussed.

In many cases, the person is determined to return home and quite a lot can be done to achieve this. Physical barriers can be removed by, for example, building a down stairs lavatory. Home helps and district nurses can be provided and neighbours often rally round. Even a profound aphasia need not prevent a person living alone.

In other cases, returning home may not be the best option. This seemed the case for Rachel:

> Shortly after Rachel was transferred to the Rehabilitation centre we began thinking about the future. One of the reasons for her stay at the centre was the need for professional assessment of her likely progress in speech and mobility. However, it was apparent that even if Rachel made excellent progress it would be difficult for her to return to her own flat. Although alterations could be made inside the flat, the many steps and stairs inside and out would present serious problems. But the deciding factor was the position of the flat which was a considerable distance from the city centre. If Rachel was to receive visitors and maintain contact with friends and colleagues she would have to live close to museums and galleries and be easily reached by public transport.
>
> After several weeks assessment the doctor concluded that Rachel was unlikely to improve and the speech and language therapist agreed. Rachel would need help and supervision twenty four hours a day. The possibility of living in a flat was unrealistic as, apart from the daunting prospect of organising and supervising staff, it did not seem prudent for someone with her very limited communication to live

alone. Our main concern was Rachel's inability to use the telephone. How would we know if staff failed to arrive? How would we know if she was distressed or in danger? So the decision to look for a nursing home was not a difficult one.

All these were negative reasons for choosing a nursing home, but there were positive reasons too. First and foremost, if Rachel were not to become too frustrated and depressed she would need continual social and intellectual stimulation. With the nursing home taking responsibility for her physical needs her friends would be able to remain *friends* and not become 'carers'. The time spent with Rachel could be used to keep her up to date with her own special interests, to play games and to provide her with enjoyable activities to occupy her when she was alone. By the time Rachel left the Rehabilitation centre it seemed wise for us to resume our own lives and to maintain our own interests and activities. As it was necessary to plan for years ahead, it was essential to contain inevitable feelings of guilt and refuse to become totally absorbed in the day-to-day problems of care. No one can deny that dealing with people who have profound communication problems such as jargon aphasia is extremely exhausting. We decided that it was more important for us to facilitate the provision of social and cultural activities rather than concentrate on physical care.

Once the nursing home decision was made, we set about creating an environment which reflected Rachel's personality and, above all, was within her control. From home we brought books, pictures, a rug and her favourite chair. Next to her chair stood her trolley:

> The trolley symbolised the heart of Rachel's world. She could organise it and make sure all she needed

had a special position on it: kleenex, spoon, napkin, lipsalve, yoghurt and petit filou for tea, a banana, water and glass, a tub of pens and pencils, the visitors' book under the diary and chocolates for guests. On the shelf below was the lap tray and a variety of magazines and sales catalogues, none too heavy to handle. At the far end, her paint satchel hung and next to that was the left-hand glove for use when walking with a tripod.

Rachel's life in the nursing home was governed by a strict routine which she fiercely protected.

Every day, Rachel walked through to breakfast. If anything was missing on the meal table Rachel soon indicated it. The problem was to find out *what* was missing. The test was like a Kim's game. Each object had its place in front of her and each stage of the meal its prescribed order. The coffee should not appear before the yoghurt had been eaten, the toast must be neither too hard nor too soft.

Deviations from the routine caused a mini crisis:

Rachel's bedside table was meticulously organised, with everything not only in its particular place but also facing a particular direction. On one occasion, I moved the bedside clock, so that it could be seen from Rachel's chair during the day. This helpfully intended act caused consternation. Only when I had moved the clock back to its customary position, facing the wall, did Rachel calm down.

Rachel's insistence on routine could be for a number of reasons. Strokes can cause personality changes and make people more rigid in their behaviours. It is possible that this happened to Rachel. However, there are other explanations. Rachel's world was turned upside down. By imposing routine, she could lessen some of the her fears and create a secure, safe environment. Her routines also gave her autonomy. Indeed, behaviours which seemed irrational or obsessional, were in fact driven by the desire to retain control over her life:

Rachel's chair occupied a precise position in her room. If it was moved even a centimetre Rachel became furious. For a while, we thought this was just Rachel 'being difficult'. Then the truth dawned. Rachel had placed her chair in the best position to see through the doorway into the passage outside. At meal times she could monitor the steady procession of residents in wheelchairs and on frames making their way to the dining hall. Only when this progression ceased would Rachel set off. In this way she ensured that her route was cleared and she could walk unobstructed into lunch.

As this example shows, Rachel's routines were often the result of a careful calculation. She had worked out the best way of coping with numerous tricky situations. It is hardly surprising that when we interfered with her solutions, she responded with outrage.

It is important that care staff understand the individual's routine and have respect for it. This was an issue for Rachel:

> Rachel's strict routines could be a source of friction with new care staff. Some care workers were more adaptable than others and learned to cope quickly and humorously with her rigid habits, thus establishing happy relationships. Others no doubt found her strange ways incomprehensible. One evening at bed time Rachel became very distressed and the staff, very concerned, thought of several possible reasons for her tears. Eventually someone realised that the clock had been removed from her bedside table. Once it was restored to its proper place Rachel said 'aah', smiled happily and went to sleep.

This example illustrates the need for continuity of care. Rachel's distress was only alleviated by a member of staff who was very familiar with the arrangement of her room and with her need for stability. Given that such continuity is not always possible to achieve, the example also shows the need for new staff to be briefed in great detail about the needs of each individual resident.

Of course, routines cannot always be adhered to, and there are occasions when necessary changes have to be introduced. Over the years, Rachel's friends learnt the best means of managing this:

> Changes of routine, discussions about plans or visitors were best dealt with in the mornings. Such changes and arrangements had to be repeated several times. Changes were accepted provided they were not unexpected. It was important for all alterations, appointments and activities to be entered in Rachel's diary, if possible well in advance. We explained to staff that Rachel's diary was not private and everyone was urged to consult it.
>
> Because we could not understand what Rachel was asking us it would have been only too easy to assume that she had no questions and that she was not thinking, interpreting and misinterpreting what was happening to her and around her. For this reason we tried to explain who people were, the reasons for visits and for all medical procedures as carefully as possible. By preparing her for all situations we hoped to prevent uncertainty, misunderstanding and fear. Even so, we were aware that if Rachel could have done so she would have told us of occasions when she had been apprehensive or distressed because of someone's failure to explain a change of plan or an unexpected medical test.

Many other people with aphasia make use of diaries and calendars. When reading is impossible, non-verbal equivalents can be developed. For example, the person might have a number of pictures symbolising the main events in their life which can be stuck onto the relevant days on a calendar.

Although Rachel valued her routine, there was little doubt that she was also frustrated and bored by the restrictions of her new life. The nursing home provided quite a wide range of activities, such as crafts and music and movement, as well as the ubiquitous bingo. Yet, none of these were interesting for Rachel and she resolutely refused to join in. One provision was ideal. This was the Arts Interest Group, founded by Mrs Joy Willey in Wandsworth.* Using specially adapted mini buses, Mrs Willey organised regular visits to galleries and museums for disabled and house bound residents of Wandsworth. Such visits were among the highlights of Rachel's life in the nursing home and for several days after each visit she showed her visitors brochures and post cards from the exhibitions she had visited.

Undoubtedly holidays right away from the nursing home gave Rachel the most enjoyment. First of all there was the pleasure of anticipation, the checking of dates in her diary, the talk about travel arrangements and decisions about packing. Then when she arrived there was the stimulus from seeing old and new friends, from eating meals with lively conversation going on round her and of visits to places of interest. And on returning to the nursing home there were albums of photographs to show visitors and staff.

Friends were often surprised by these holidays, given the extent of Rachel's disabilities. However, with meticulous staff work and a good deal of resilience on Rachel's part, travelling even quite long distances was possible:

---

* After a number of years, this group has now been taken over by Age Concern, Wandsworth

When friends heard that we took Rachel to France for holidays we were usually asked, ' How do you manage?' Well, first of all we planned each stage of the journey very carefully and did our best to avoid surprises. Then we always took Rachel to the same place where she felt at home and where she knew the neighbours and the physiotherapist. It was a house with many happy memories for her. We entered the dates of her departure and her return in her diary several weeks beforehand and often referred to our holiday plans.

We travelled by air because it was fast and, to get to the airport, we travelled by taxi. We also allowed plenty of time for delays on the road and in order to check in early. On arriving at the airport, one encountered a potentially serious problem if travelling alone with Rachel. Because she was unable to walk long distances she travelled in her wheelchair. This meant that whoever was accompanying her was responsible both for the wheelchair and a luggage trolley. If porters were available this solved the problem. If not, Rachel did, by gamely propelling the wheelchair through the crowds with her left foot.

Once at the check-in desk staff were usually helpful and willingly arranged for someone to push the wheelchair to the departure lounge and finally on to the plane. Here the wheelchair was taken away to join the luggage and Rachel walked to her seat. As she had the use of only one hand and was unable to communicate with staff, it was essential for her and her friend to sit together near the front of the plane. As a rule, check-in staff made this possible.

Fortunately Rachel had travelled all over the world before her stroke and consequently she was used to airports, to customs and to delays. On her first trip abroad after her stroke she was a little anxious until she reached the plane, but after the first journey out she accepted any problems cheerfully. Like all of us,

Rachel had a fear of the unknown and with her this natural anxiety was increased by an awareness that she was unable to control any situation. For this reason we tried to make travelling, whether to the dentist or to France, as predicable as possible.

One of the biggest problems we faced after Rachel's stroke was her inability to express her feelings about her situation. Although Rachel could not voice her feelings, others in similar situations, have. Reading these personal accounts of stroke has been invaluable. Through them we have been given a glimpse of what Rachel might say if only her jargon would subside.

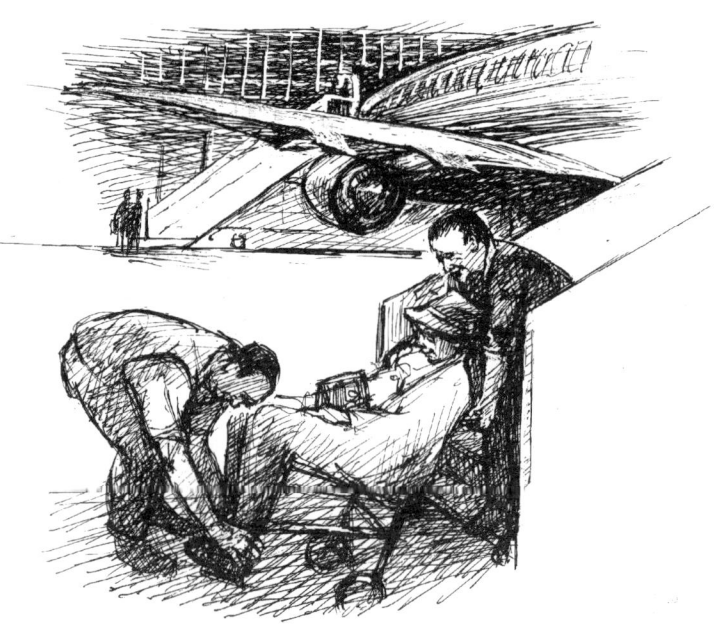

Final Thoughts

'Even though I am so much better now, I am changed forever,' Robert McCrumb

For several weeks following Rachel's stroke when acquaintances heard about the extent of her disabilities they commented that it would have been better if she had died. But against all the odds she recovered and it was necessary for us to look to the future. Although we soon recognised many of the personality traits of the old Rachel, such as her tenacity, her determination and her intolerance of what she regarded as stupidity, we knew that the old Rachel had gone for ever. It was essential for us to learn to understand the new Rachel.

As she could not communicate verbally we could only deduce from her behaviour her emotional and intellectual reaction to her predicament. It was obvious that she often became desperately frustrated and angry. In the early months we realised that she also had a fear of being abandoned. So, we demonstrated that we would not abandon her; that we could be trusted. And we dealt with her new insecurity by explaining all plans carefully and repeatedly. Once we realised that she retained her interest in her professional skills, we began to provide her with suitable publications and to discuss these with her.

As she settled in the nursing home and gained confidence, the old Rachel could be observed helping those more timid or more disabled than herself, protesting about an unmade bed or sharing a joke with a care assistant. Within her small world, and in spite of the fact that she was almost entirely dependent on the help of others, she managed to assert herself and maintain some independence.

Surprisingly, after her stroke Rachel was more relaxed socially, losing some of her reserve with strangers and, despite her profound problems in communication, welcoming opportunities to meet people. And so, in some ways, Rachel had changed, and unquestionably her life had changed dramatically. In many respects this was a new Rachel, living a new, not uninteresting life, but a new life nevertheless.

Glossary

Aphasia
: Aphasia is a language disorder usually caused by stroke or head injury. Technically, aphasia means the total loss of language, while dysphasia refers to partial loss. However, the terms tend to be used interchangeably.

    Most people with aphasia have damage on the left side of the brain, as this is where the structures which process language are located. However, occasionally right sided damage can cause aphasia, particularly if the person is left handed.

    Aphasia disrupts all aspects of language, ie speaking, understanding, reading and writing. It can also limit the person's use of non-verbal symbols, such as gesture or drawing. Other mental skills are unaffected. Aphasic people can still solve problems, remember and think of ideas. Their problem is in communicating those ideas.

Articulatory Dyspraxia
: See Dyspraxia

Dysarthria
: Dysarthria is a speech problem due either to muscle paralysis or to an impairment in the nerves which supply the speech muscles. Causes of dysarthria include stroke, progressive brain diseases, and muscle disorders, such as muscular dystrophy. Dysarthria varies in severity. Some people have slurred, indistinct speech, while others are completely unintelligible. Unlike aphasia, dysarthria is not a language problem, so dysarthric people can still understand speech, read and write

(providing there are no other problems). Dysarthric people can often be helped by communication aids, such as speech synthesises. A familiar user of such an aid is the scientist Stephen Hawking.

Dysgraphia   Acquired Dysgraphia is a disorder of writing usually caused by damage to the left side of the brain. Most aphasic people have dysgraphia, at least to some extent. However, in some cases writing may be more intact than speech.

It should be stressed that dysgraphia is a *language* problem and not simply a difficulty with the mechanics of writing. This is important, because many people with dysgraphia also have a paralysis of their right hand. Relatives may therefore believe that the writing problem is due to this paralysis. However, this is not the case. People with dysgraphia show spelling difficulties even when attempting to write with their left hand and people with no paralysis can still be dysgraphic. Dysgraphic people also have difficulty assembling words from scrabble tiles. It seems that people with dysgraphia can no longer recall how words should be written.

Dyslexia   Dyslexia is a reading impairment. Most people are now familiar with the term when it is applied to children who have a particular problem learning to read (Developmental Dyslexia). Less familiar is Acquired Dyslexia, which refers to the loss of established reading ability following brain damage. Most aphasic people also have some degree of acquired dyslexia.

Research has shown that there are different patterns of acquired dyslexia, which particularly affect certain classes of words. Many dyslexic people find it difficult to read grammatical words (such as 'the' or 'was'), which is surprising given that these words are very short and extremely common. Abstract words (such as 'idea' or democracy') can also cause problems, as can words with irregular spellings (such as 'yacht' and 'mortgage'). The speech and language therapist will attempt to assess reading in order to find out which words can still be read and understood.

Dysphagia   Dysphagia refers to a problem with swallowing. It can occur after strokes because the nerve supply to the muscles in the mouth and throat has been disrupted. Often, the dysphagia is only a temporary problem. However, in some cases the difficulty persists. If the problem is very severe, eating may no longer be possible. In this case the person may be fed through a tube passing directly into the stomach.

Dysphagia requires urgent management, not only for nutritional reasons, but also because the problem can result in food and liquid dropping into the air way and lungs. Surprisingly, speech and language therapists are involved in the assessment and treatment of dysphagia, mainly because they are very informed about oral structures and movement.

Dysphasia   See Aphasia

Dyspraxia
(also termed
Apraxia)   Dyspraxia is a puzzling condition which impairs the co-ordination of planned movements.

There are different forms of dyspraxia, affecting different types of movement. One form is Articulatory Dyspraxia. As the name implies this affects the co-ordination of speech movements.

Dyspraxia is not due to paralysis of the muscles. So someone with articulatory dyspraxia will still be able to perform a range of oral movements (such as eating and yawning). They may even be able to produce highly automatic speech (such as swearing and counting). Their difficulties only emerge when trying to produce planned speech. Dyspraxia can co-exist with dysphasia. However, it is not present in jargon aphasia, where speech movement is fluent and effortless.

Hemianopia A hemianopia is the loss of perception in half the field of vision. Hemianopias are not due to a problem in the eyes. Rather, they occur when the part of the brain which processes vision has been damaged. The affected area of vision depends on the site of the brain damage, with right sided damage causing a left hemianopia and left sided damage causing a right hemianopia. Some aphasic people have a hemianopia. If this is the case, the hemianopia usually affects the right visual field.

People with hemianopia cannot see objects or people on the affected side. So a person with a right hemianopia may not notice their glasses if they are placed on the right side of a table in front of them, or may react with exaggerated surprise when someone approaches them from the right. For this reason, rehabilitation staff often remind hemianopic people to turn their heads more to the affected side to compensate for the problem.

Hemiplegia Hemiplegia is a paralysis affecting one side of the body. It is caused by brain damage, such as stroke or head injury.

The affected side of the body is determined by the location of the brain damage. Surprisingly, right hemiplegia is caused by left sided brain damage, while left hemiplegia is caused by right sided damage. This is because the nerve pathways which control movement 'cross over' in the neck.

Hemiplegias vary in severity. For example, some people retain some movement in the hemiplegic leg even though the arm is useless; while others are unable to use both limbs. Many people with hemiplegia learn to walk again, with the assistance of physiotherapy. Others require the long term use of a wheelchair.

Jargon Aphasia In Jargon Aphasia speech is fluent but very difficult to understand. Jargon speech varies. In some cases, it is constructed mainly from real words, although in very anomalous combinations. In others, there are frequent non words or neologisms. Jargon speakers often produce sentences, or sentence like strings of speech, although these may contain grammatical errors. Commonly, people with jargon aphasia also have severe problems understanding speech and have difficulties with reading and writing. Many jargon speakers also have very poor awareness of their speech problems.

Jargon aphasia is sometimes referred to as Wernicke's Aphasia after Carl Wernicke the nineteenth-century German neurologist who first described the syndrome.

Occupational Therapy
Occupational therapists work with a range of clients with physical and cognitive disabilities.

Following stroke, occupational therapists aim to help the person resume a range of daily activities and functions. For example, they may help with self caring skills, such as washing, dressing and cooking or may advise about mobility (usually in collaboration with the physiotherapists). Occupational therapists are usually very involved in helping the person return home after a stroke, eg they will assess the person's needs and advise about any aids and adaptations.

Physiotherapy
Physiotherapists are concerned with the remediation of a wide range of physical disabilities, in both children and adults.

Following stroke, physiotherapists are most involved in the rehabilitation of any paralysis or hemiplegia. Targets for therapy may include: re-establishing sitting balance, enabling the person to stand and walking practice. The physio will also aim to prevent harmful movement patterns, which might increase the person's problems, from being established.

Speech and Language Therapy
Speech and language therapists are concerned with the remediation of communication problems in children and adults. They work with a wide range of clients, including children with language delay and disorder, people with learning

difficulties, people with physical disabilities and, of course, people who have had strokes.

Speech and language therapists are involved in a number of aspects of stroke rehabilitation. In the early days, they may assess and treat any swallowing difficulties (see dysphagia). This aspect of their work often surprises relatives, but arose because speech and language therapists are very informed about oral movements and structures.

The principal role of the speech and language therapist is to assess and provide therapy for the communication difficulties following stroke. Aphasia therapy takes many forms. It may aim to re-establish lost language skills, or to compensate for them. For example, if the person cannot speak, the therapist may encourage them to use gesture or drawing to convey their ideas as well as trying to restore a useful spoken vocabulary. We are still developing our understanding of aphasia and how to treat it. Many aphasic people, like Rachel, contribute to this enterprise by generously participating in therapy research.

For more information about speech and language therapy contact: The Royal College of Speech and Language Therapists, 7 Bath Place, Rivington Street, London EC2A 3DR.

Stroke   A stroke, or Cerebrovascular Accident, occurs when the blood supply to the brain is partially cut off, resulting in damage to some of the brain tissue. Strokes have different causes.

In some cases a blood clot obstructs circulation, while in others a blood vessel within the brain ruptures, causing a bleed or haemorrhage.

Strokes can result in a variety of disabilities, depending on the site and extent of the brain damage. Common difficulties are: paralysis (see hemiplegia), speech and language problems (see aphasia, dysarthria and dyspraxia) and visual problems (see hemianopia). In some cases these problems improve or even resolve over time. In others, there is a permanent disability.

Action for Dysphasic Adults produce an excellent leaflet explaining strokes, which is designed for dysphasic people. It is called 'Stroke and Dysphasia: drawing the picture together'.

Bibliography

Bauby J-D (1997) *The Diving Bell and the Butterfly.* London: Fourth Estate

Jones Trevor (1997) *Walking on Air.* Heinemann

McCrumb R (1998) *My Year Off: Rediscovering Life after Stroke.* London: Picador

Parr S, Byng S, and Gilpin S (1997) *Talking about Aphasia: Living with Loss of Language after Stroke.* Milton Keynes: Open University Press

Parr S, Pound C, Byng S and Long S (1999) *The Aphasia Handbook.* CONNECT press. Available from: Ecodistribution, 117 Main Street, Woodhouse Eaves, Leicestershire, LE12 8RY

Helpful Organisations

Action for Dysphasic Adults. 1 Royal Street, London SE1 7LL. Tel: (020) 7261 9572

Different Strokes. Sir Walter Scott House, 2 Broadway Market, London E8 4QJ. Tel: (020) 7249 6645

The Stroke Association. Stroke House, Whitecross Street, London EC1Y 8JJ. Tel: (020) 7490 2686